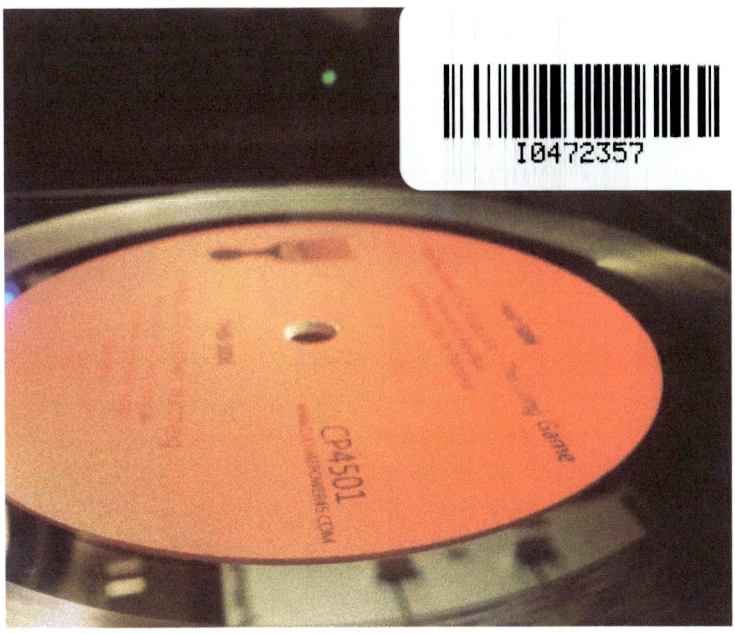

I0472357

Culture Power45 is a Label Exclusively for
Vinyl. Culture Power 45 is a source grounded
in providing culturally based sound to a
worldwide audience via the limited and
collectible vinyl format. We believe in our
mission of empowering the people through
music so the people can power the culture!
www.culturepower45.com

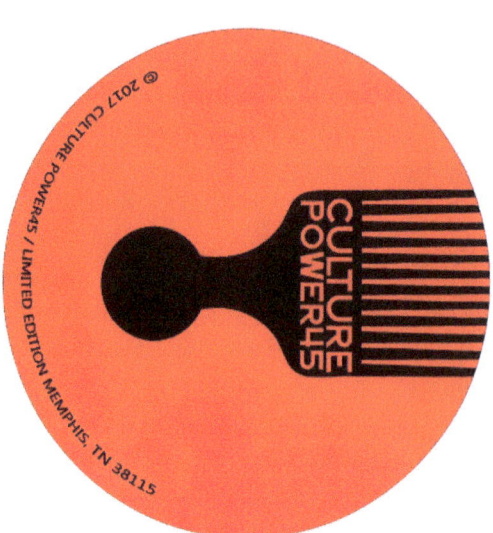

© 2017 CULTURE POWER45 / LIMITED EDITION MEMPHIS, TN 38115

CULTURE POWER45

CULTURE
POWER45

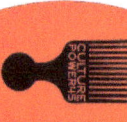

CULTURE POWER45

THAT SIDE

MaxPtah featuring Blueprint - The Long Game

Produced by MaxPtah

artistTREE Ent. / Dig Ink Publishing

THIS SIDE

Infinito 2017 - Brothers Watching

Produced by The Deity Complex

M. Lovelace (Infinito One / Ascap)

+ bonus beats

CP4501

WWW.CULTUREPOWER45.COM

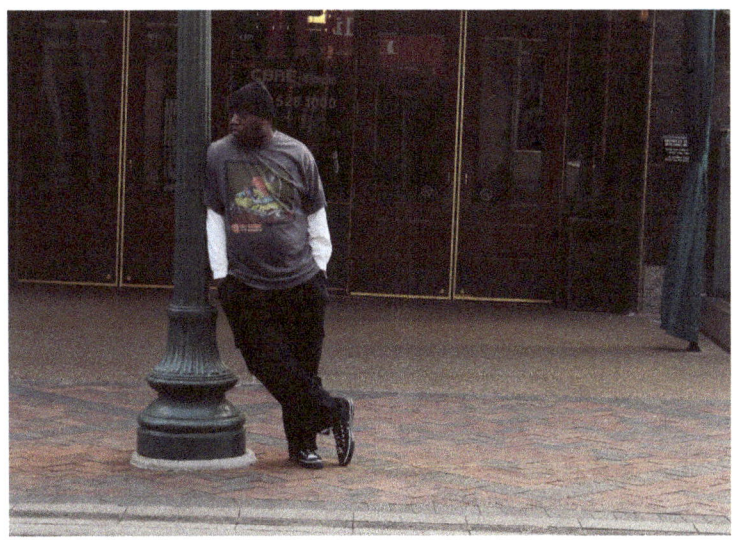

MAXPTAH

MEMPHIS, TN

MaxPtah is a recording artist and Hip Hop producer out of
Memphis, TN. As an astute student of the culture MaxPtah
has been able to round out his sound to expand beyond the
genre of Hip Hop to Soul, Neo-Soul, Funk, and House
music, but Hip Hop is his foundation and his home.
MaxPtah is an avid record collector and has built a
modest collection of albums that he uses as a source of
inspiration and also enjoyment. He also shoots and edits
his own music videos and videos for others as well. In
2011 he was nominated for a Viewer's Choice Award in Live
from Memphis's Music Video Showcase for the song "All I
Need". MaxPtah was the only video director in the whole
showcase that had no formal training/education in
shooting or editing. It was his vision and drive to put
the best product out that brought the video to life.

Discography

Memphite Theology - 2005
Life, Love, Respect, & Hip Hop - 2007
Absolute Zero EP - 2008
Empee & MaxPtah "Listen" - 2009
Best in the World - 2011
Live From Everywhere - 2014
Full Range Frequency - 2016

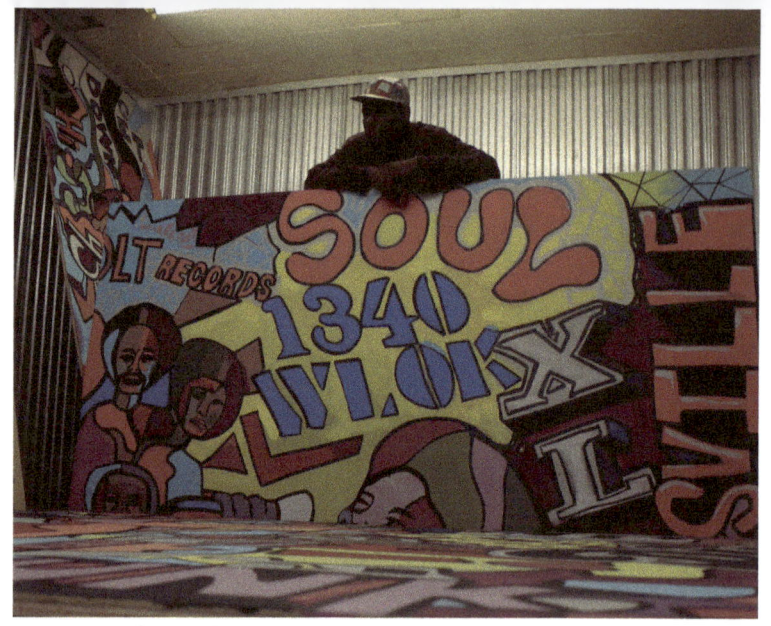

Infinito 2017

CHICAGO, IL

Infinito 2017 was Born October 26, in Chicago,
Marcellous Lamont Lovelace: Broadcasting the most
interesting Hip Hop Music you've ever heard in your
life. Teaching and informing African people (and others)
about Self Esteem, Awareness, Determination, Fighting
Against Tricknology, Freedom Fighting, Nationalism,
Skills, Making New music on a constant basis to allow
for better free thought with over 200 albums recorded
and 10,000 paintings and counting. www.infinito2017.com

Discography (To Long To List)

1998 Infinito / Documentary LP Egruks / Nephew of Frank
1998 Unorthodox Poets Society / left hand Jim Crow papers
1998 Infinito / vol. 843 Nephew of Frank
1999 Infinito / year of the rabbit Egruks/Nephew of Frank
2000 Unusuall Situation Association / who voted for bush?
2001 Unorthodox Poets Society presents: Elongated Testicle EP
2001 Unorthodox Poets Society / slightly conjugated 351
2001 Infinito presents: oneINDIVISUAL no reason Nephew of Frank
2004 Infinito vs. Molemen Mixtape HES DEFINITLY NOT IN THE BUILDING
2004 I.T. (INFINITO AND THAIONE) LOW INCOME HOUSING Domination
2005 oneINDIVISUAL / VOICE NEEDED Nephew of frank
2005 INFINITO 2017/ EYE ELEVATE Nephew of Frank
2007 Infinito 2017 / Shes In The Wind / Nephew of Frank
2007 Infinito 2017 / Nephew Of Frank / Nephew of Frank
2007 Infinito 2017 / This Is A Day Unlike Others / Nephew of Frank
2009 Ka Sekhem / Sense of Urgency: Nubian Love
2009 Marcellous Lovelace / Happiness Disposition
2009 Infinito 2017 - Divine Love
2009 Infinito 2017 Day Of The Night
2012 Nekaybaaw & Ka Sekhem - Of Unknown Origin
2012 The Square Pyramid (Ardamus + Infinito 2017) - The Square Pyramid
2012 Infinito 2017 - Never Artificial / Not You (Who) (7 inch)
2012 Colored Black - A Tear For My People
2012 Infinito 2017 - Quality in Quantity
2013 Marcellous Lovelace - Exposed Erotions in Color
2013 Vortx of Distorsun - BIKO BANIU CONGO LUMMBA
2014 Infinito 2017 - Threatening Music X Brash and Abrasive
2014 Infinito 2017 - Single Consciousness My Independent Mine
2015 Marcellous Lovelace - Reduce Noise (Instrumental)
2015 Infinito 2017 - AntiEverything (Tape also)
2015 Marcellous Lovelace - death of Old English saturn
2015 Marcellous Lovelace - Condemned Buildings Part GS
2016 Infinito 2017 - I MELANIN DARK SKIN
2016 Infinito 2017 - Not Parts Of Your Watu (10" vinyl EP)
2016 Marcellous Lovelace - Apala Mejuputara Uda
2016 ML7102 - Enhanced Movements Out East
2016 ML7102 - readings of a unwanted story
2016 ML7102 - Night Late Complexion

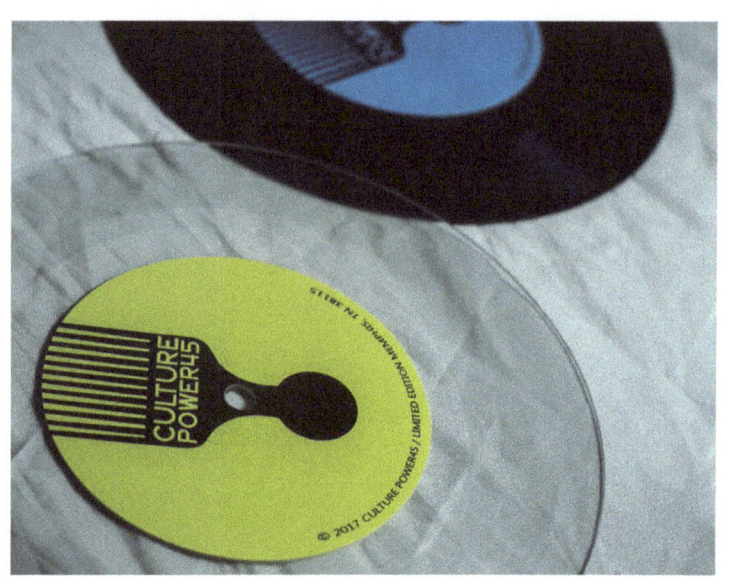

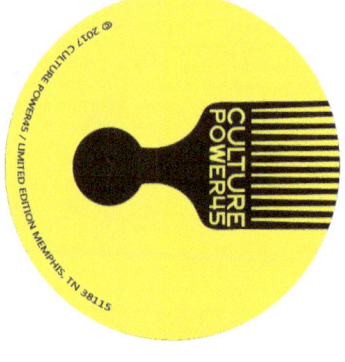

CULTURE POWER45

℗ 2017 CULTURE POWER45 / LIMITED EDITION MEMPHIS, TN 38115

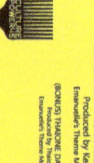

THAT SIDE

Thaione Davis - 85 Brokers (tumbleweeds mix)
Produced by Kenny Keys
Ensemble's Theme Music (ASCAP)

(BONUS) THAIONE DAVIS - Subville
Produced by Thaione Davis
Ensemble's Theme Music (ASCAP)

THIS SIDE

JASON THE HATER - Stuff of Local Legend
Produced by EMPEE
Recorded by Maayah

CP4502
WWW.CULTUREPOWER45.COM

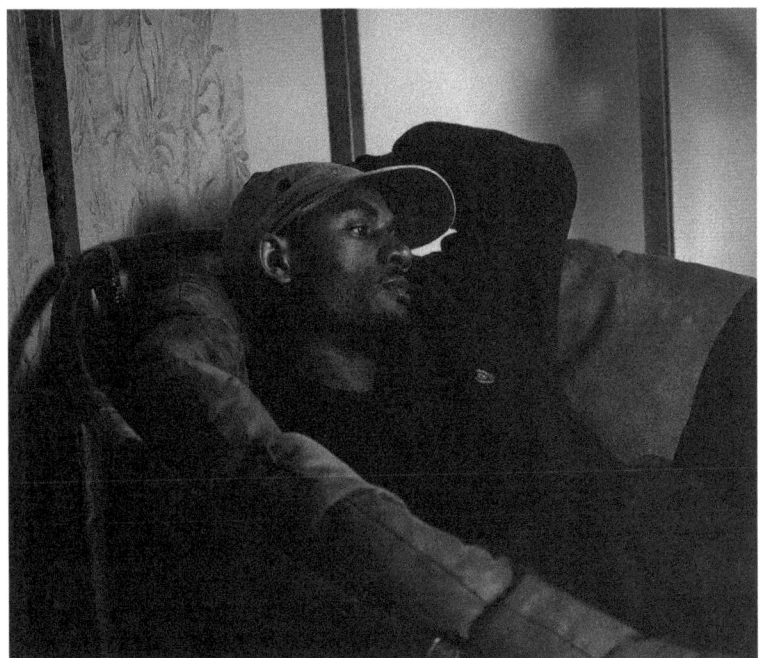

Thaione Davis

CHICAGO, IL

As an accomplished producer/emcee born and raised on the Southside of
Chicago, Davis has silently become a vessel in the ranks of hip hop
domestic and abroad. With several releases on both sides of the
water, Thaione has developed a niche for capturing the many moods and
passions of life. A true renaissance contemporary with multi
disciplines ranging from photography, to design and engineering.
Modest by nature, meticulous by trade, Davis thoroughly embodies the
essence before an innocence lost. www.thaionedavis.com

Discography

PROGRESS 2.6
APRIL JANUARY
SITUATION RENAISSANCE
ELEPHANT BEACH
QUALITY CONTROL
BURGUNDY (THE ANTEBELLUM COLLECTION)
COMPOSURE
STILL HEAR
GOODENOUGH
SEVENTEEN
EMANUELLE'S THEME MUSIC
THE JOYS OF LIFE & PAIN
ACKNOWLEDGE PAIN
WALKING ANONYMOUS
DONALD MAYHEM - SKYWRITTERS

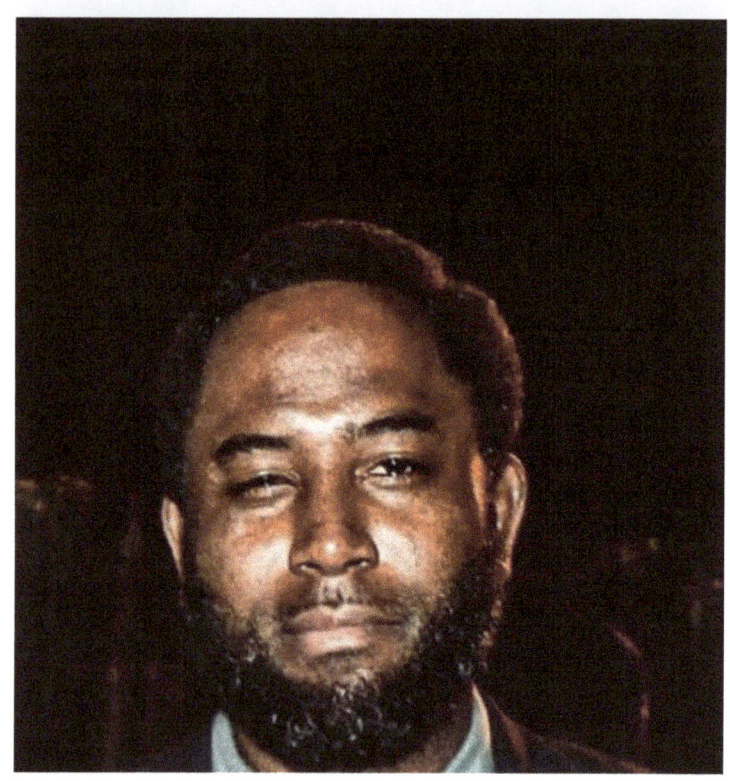

Jason Da Hater

MEMPHIS, TN

Memphop agent, code name Da Hater/ girls with a terrible grill, I'll never date ya/ won't touch your broad, even though she goin'/ my trash talk will ruin yo team like Terrell Owens/ Rap game participant/ relentless when I'm in this, mention this/ I vent and represent for my constituents/ this Memphis resident/ speak this testament/ it's evident I'm heaven sent/ hard to break or dent/ I never quit.........plus I'm an aspiring bear hunter....Da hater

Discography

Hating in its finest Hour
The Worst Best Rapper in Town (Mix tape)
Enough Hate to Go Around
Like Vegetables E.P.
You're A Nation, Number 1 Flow (Mix tape)
You're-N-Trouble, King of Memphis Flow (Mix tape)
Hate and Hip Hop Season 12

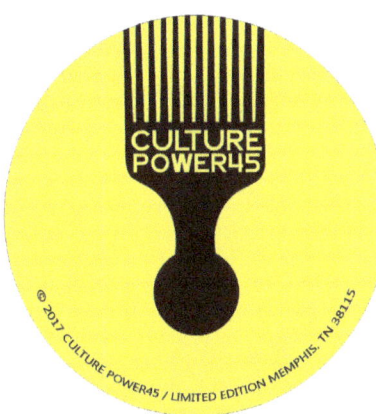

© 2017 CULTURE POWER45 / LIMITED EDITION MEMPHIS, TN 38115

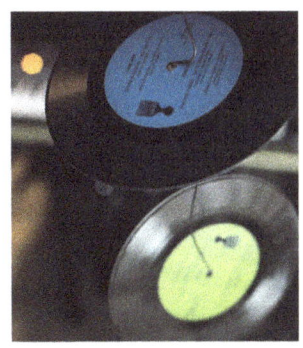

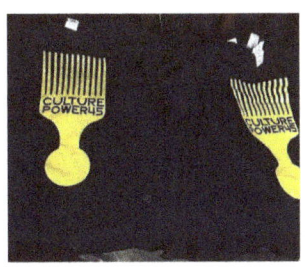

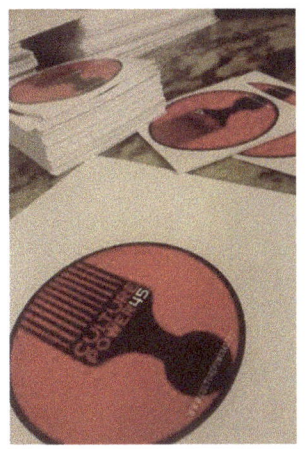

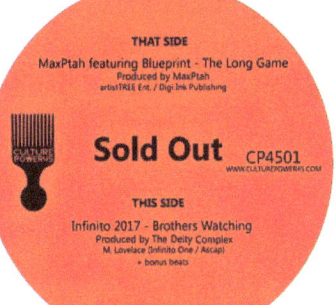

THAT SIDE

MaxPtah featuring Blueprint - The Long Game
Produced by MaxPtah
artistTREE Ent. / Digi Ink Publishing

Sold Out CP4501
WWW.CULTUREPOWER45.COM

THIS SIDE

Infinito 2017 - Brothers Watching
Produced by The Deity Complex
M. Lovelace (Infinito One / Ascap)
+ bonus beats

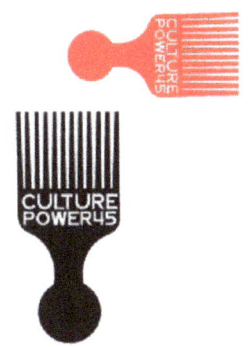

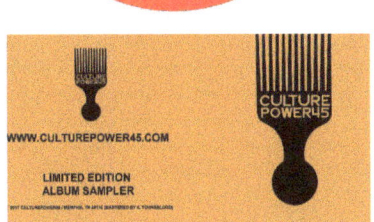

WWW.CULTUREPOWER45.COM

**LIMITED EDITION
ALBUM SAMPLER**

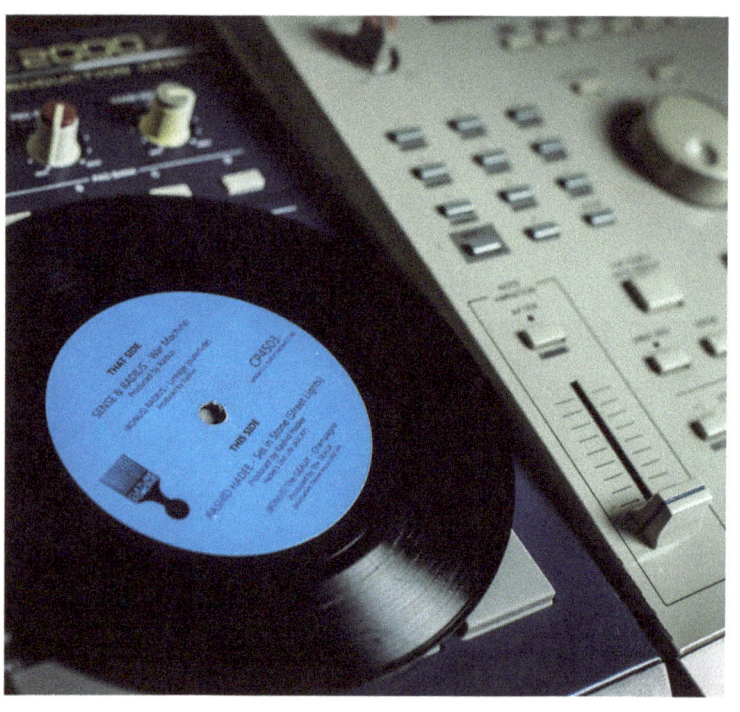

THAT SIDE

SENSE & RADIUS - War Machine
Produced by Radius

(BONUS) RADIUS - Lineage (outerlude)
Produced by Radius

THIS SIDE

RASHID HADEE - Set in Stone (Street Lights)
Produced by Rashid Hadee
Hadee's 2nd Life ASCAP

(BONUS) The GEAUX - Champagne
Produced by The GEAUX
SMI/CROWN THEME MUSIC (ASCAP)

CP4503

WWW.CULTUREPOWER45.COM

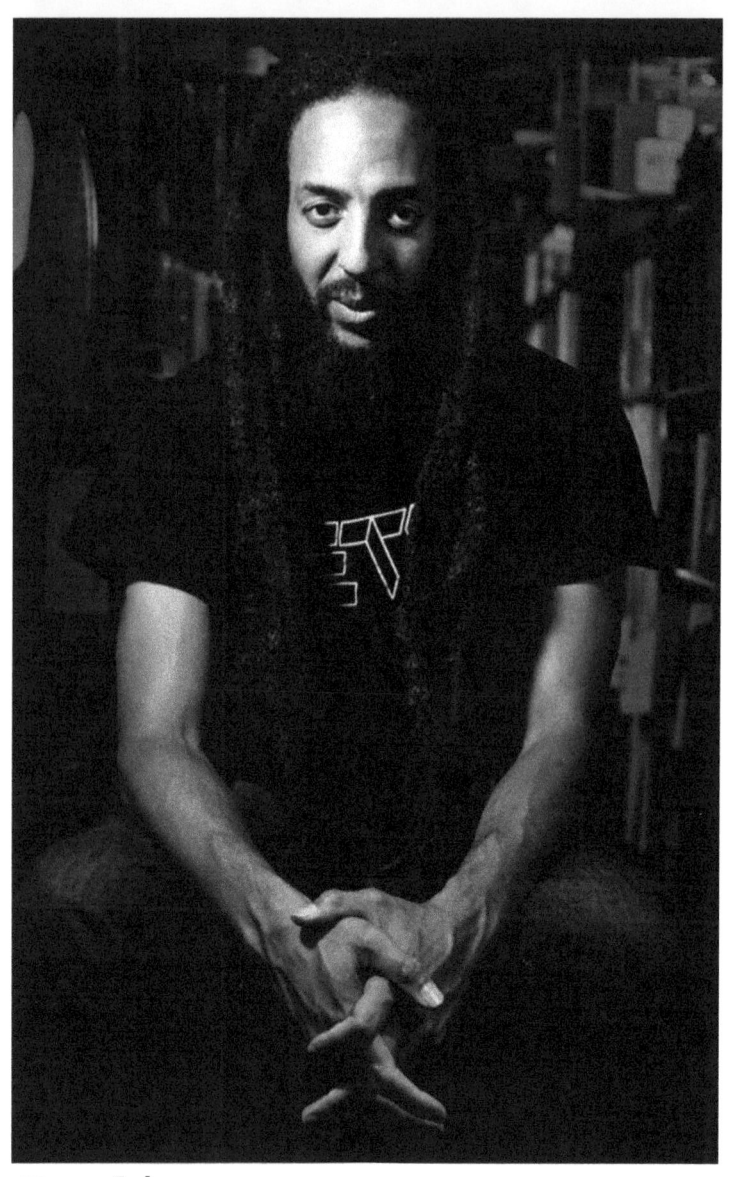

Radius

CHICAGO, IL

A focused multi-dimensional "post-genre" based artist from South Chicago; Radius started crafting beats in 2001. After producing tracks for local rappers, he began to further hone his skills as a producer/live performance artist, by winning in Chicago area beat battles and later performing in various hiphop & electronic showcases with the Moment Sound Crew (Garo, Lokua & Slava). Radius is known for his improv hardware live PA/beat sets; which range from a wide variety of tempos & sounds, highly inspired by his hip-hop, jazz, dub & house music roots; due to his Chicago upbringing.

Radius has rocked alongside noteworthy artists including; Dj Shadow, Nightmares On Wax, Anderson Paak, Daedelus, Oddisee, Blu & Exile, RC and The Gritz Band (Erykah Badu) Eliot Lipp, Mndsgn,The Gaslamp Killer, Thavius Beck, Jeremiah Jae, Ras G, Mono/Poly, Dj Houseshoes, & Guilty Simpson.

Notable live showcases include; Dublab (Los Angeles & Japan), B-Real TV (Los Angeles), Stop Biting Lo- Fi (Seattle), Exploded Drawing (Austin), The Beat Swap Meet (Los Angeles & Chicago), Push Beats (Chicago) Beat Cinema (Los Angeles), The Beat Haus (New York), The Low End Theory (Los Angeles), Left Field (Japan) and even hosting his own residency; Electronic Buffet, with various producers within Chicago and beyond. His 2008 debut full length CD releases; Neighborhood Suicide (The Secret Life of Sound), was well received in addition to; Radiushead, his free Radiohead remix EP released that same year. In 2009 two limited independent projects; Scatterbrain Tapes Vol. 1 (Plustapes) a local Chicago cassette based label and custom limited CD release 'Etc...' (Grittygoat) based in NYC were released, with Sleeping Wide Awake (Moment Sound) to follow in 2012. These and a few other projects showcased Radius' growth and diversity, which led to mentions in Remix magazine, The Chicago Reader, The Chicago Tribune, Pot Holes In My Blog, The Amoeba Records Blog, an interview on the Frank 151 blog, The Stranger (Seattle) and an appearance on J.Rocc's (Beat Junkies/Stonesthrow) Adventures In Stereo Radio Show on KPFK in Los Angeles.

Radius is a cofounder of various groups including; LAGOS (w/ Leo 123), Beyond Luck (w/ Dj Moppy, Kenny Keys & Lailah Reich), Dia.L (W/ Lailah Reich), Sense & Radius, Gomen (W/ Kiara Lanier & Cos) and The Present Elders (W/ Brother EL) The solo release; Time Travel Is Real, was the first vinyl pressed up on Radius' Etc Records (Ear To Chicago) imprint last September as well as vinyl from this past July, with vocalist Lailah Reich, together known as; Dia.L. Recent releases include; Infinity, a collaboration Vinyl Lp with fellow Chicago/ Beyond Luck member; Kenny Keys (Urban Waves/RadioJuicy/HHV), a split 7" with Tokyo based producer; BudaMunk from The Secret Life of Sound label, and a 12' to follow on Mathematics Recordings.

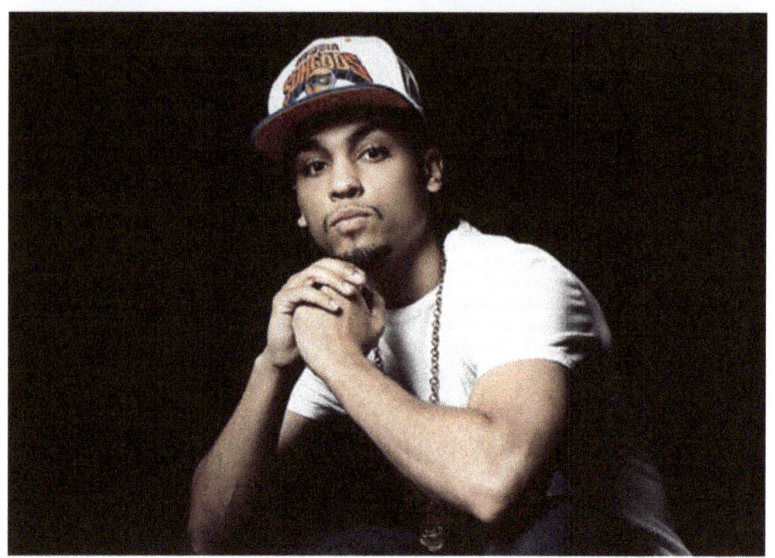

Sense

CHICAGO, IL

Born on February 17th 1989; Matt Ewing A.K.A. Sense is a Chicago native. When it comes to the mic his abilities are incredible. He can flip many schemes and styles and still manages to be sharp as sword lyrically. However, he is far more than just a rapper. He is a real master of ceremonies; truly inclined with the cultural side of hip-hop, beyond the beats and rhymes. Sense uses experiences with elements such as graffiti, rollerblading, filming, painting, and instrumental production to the fullest in the formation of his words. In about 1999, much before he even began to spit, Matt Ewing would roam the streets of Chicago on skates; jumping off and grinding on all corners of the city. Although, rollerblading is not necessarily defined as an element of hip-hop, it is still a positive culture of city life for many kids, and doesn't cost much money. Like all other extreme sports, and similar to hip-hop, booting is about style, creativity, and innovation. Like many other skaters, Matt developed a passion for filming. He and his friends would bring camcorders to skate sessions and competitions and share edits with each other. While watching rollerblade videos Matt was able to come across music that radio stations didn't play, and became captivated by underground hip-hop music. www.beatmonstas.com/artists/sense/

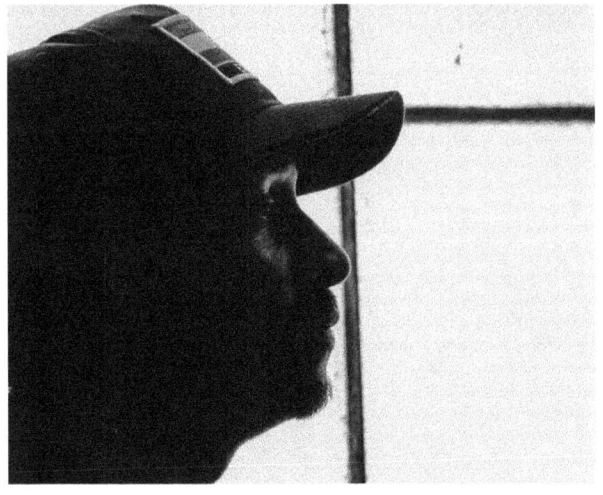

Rashid Hadee

Self-contained would be the best way to describe the producer/artist known to the world as Rashid Hadee. This Chicago native has roots that extend to Jackson, Mississippi where he began his career as a member of the mid-2000s stand out rap duo Chapter 13. He is internationally known as the go-to person when you desire hard hitting soulful beats reminiscent of rap's golden era but with a progressive, modern day feel. Legendary producers such as 9th Wonder and Erick Sermon have given the nod to Rashid Hadee's work. The adulation is very much welcomed by the beat smith being that he is strongly influenced by their work and others such as DJ Premier, J Dilla, Pete Rock, Madlib, Just Blaze and Jake One. As a producer, he has provided music for Little Brother ("Dreams"), Fashawn ("Something To Believe In" featuring Nas & Aloe Blacc), Thaione Davis, Neak, Pugs Atomz, Rita J, Tonya Morgan and many more. As a solo artist, Hadee made his introduction with the underground hit single "Surrender" and has released albums with P-Vine Records, Neblina Records, and Soulspazm Records. Andrew Barber (Fake Shore Drive) has stated, "Rashid Hadee dropped one of the dopest and most creative projects during my tenure at FSD, 808s & Hadee." Rashid Hadee is an internationally recognized double-threat musician that has been featured in XXL Magazine (Chairman's Choice), MTV, 2DopeBoyz, Fake Shore Drive, Nah Right, Ruby Hornet, Djbooth.net, Producers I Know, DJ Mag (UK), Stealth Magazine (Australia), Violator DJs, Serie B Magazine (Spain), Platform8470 and many more. The main source for music and everything related to Rashid Hadee can be found at www.rashidhadee.com and his releases are also available on all digital music streaming services.

Discography:

2015 Philmore Greene & Rashid Hadee - Get Gone (Single)(Soul 360 Entertainment)
2008 Rashid Hadee & Analogic - Serenade For The Moment (Soulspazm Records)
2007 Rashid Hadee – Dedication (Neblina Records)
2007 Rashid Hadee Surrender (Maxi-Single) (Neblina Records)
2006 Rashid Hadee - It Aint Hard To Tell (Neblina Records)
2005 Rashid Hadee - Dedication (Japan)(P-Vine Records/Blues Interactive)
2005 Chapter 13 - Nevermore's Asylum (Neblina Records)

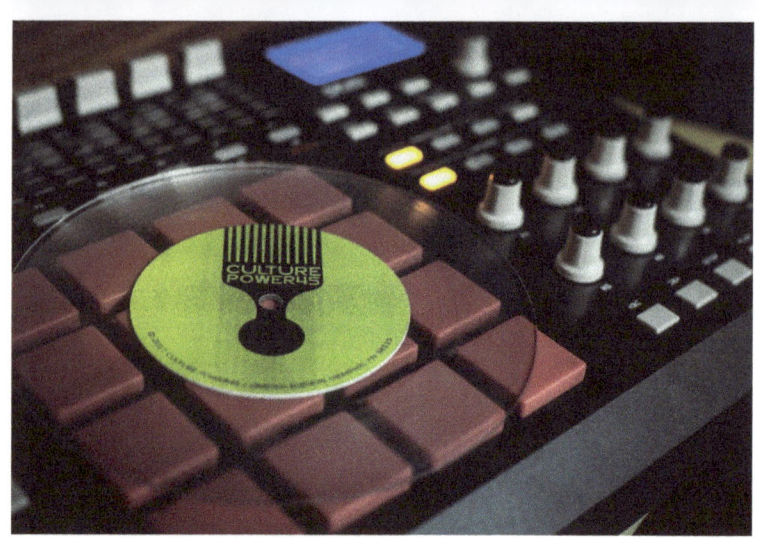

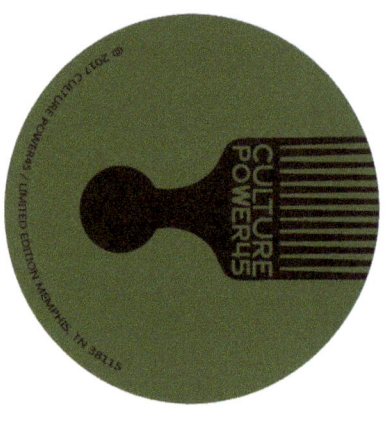

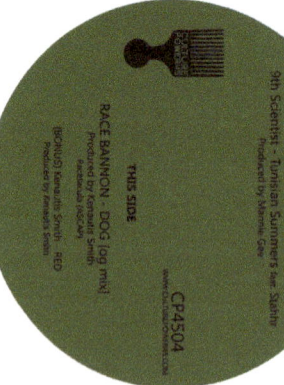

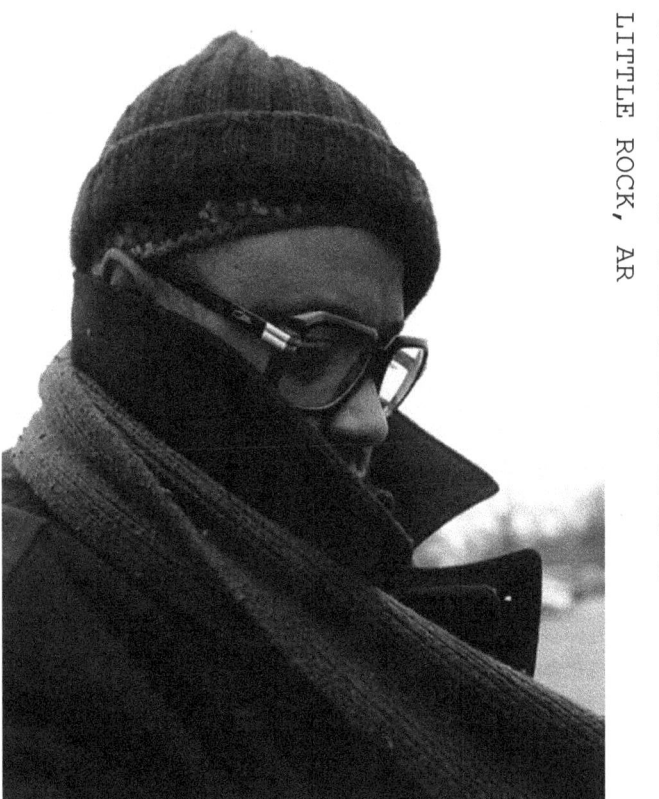

9th Scientist

LITTLE ROCK, AR

9th scientist got his start in 1991 as a part of the now defunct Hiphop collective Nubian intelligence organization. During his formative years 9th scientist recorded demos from 1991-1995 rocking underground shows with the punk rockers in Littlerock, Arkansas at Littlerocks belvedere and the punk house on rice street. 9th scientist signed to indie imprint merkabah entertainment in 1999 releasing a record under the auspice of Akasha called Kadillac Story in 2001 Produced By: THX & Swift 720. In 2002-2003 9th scientist dropped the Akasha moniker formed illatron entertainment, recorded a Seven song Ep called Cientific shot his first video the 9th episode which was released summer of 2003 during this time he started to pick up buzz from doing lots of local shows and regional touring. From 2004-2006 9th scientist started recording for the record illatron magnetic which was released in 2007 on domination recordings this record was given 4 stars in Urb magazine. This record gained critical acclaim which caught the attention of MF Grimm who made him an honorary member of monster island czars. In 2010-2011 9th Scientist followed up illatron magnetic with the release of Tru Kingz of Boom Produced by: KingBoom? In 2012 9th Scientist released follow up Record illatron archives. His latest release drops in 2014 9th scientist Neb King Cold E.P. produced By: Mannie Gee.

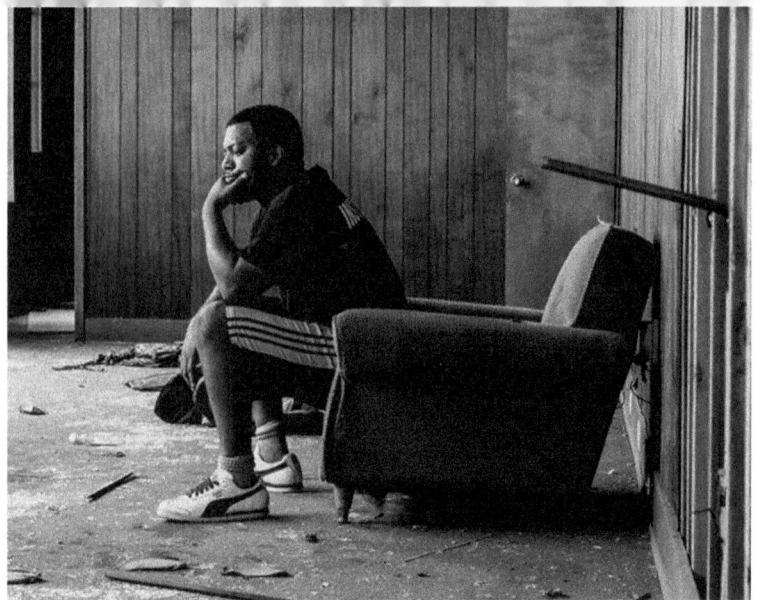

RACE BANNON

CHICAGO, IL

Race is an electrifying, captivating emcee able to entice those in
earshot with lyrical prowess, depth and a distinct, strong voice.
Race is a mix of the old + new - the new essence, a combination of
late 80s, early 90s themes done in the 21st millennium way. He's
like a loaded gun; he can go off at anytime. Come take a ride on
the soul side of the spectrum, walk with Race, hear /see something
new. Darshon "Race" Gibbs is an electrifying and captivating emcee
able to entice those in earshot with lyrical prowess, depth and a
distinct, strong voice. Born on Chicago's infamous South Side,
Race gave his first rap performance during a school play in the
7th grade. Since that day, there has been no turning back.
Determined to share his gift of poetic wit and sarcastic wisdom,
he began doing local radio shows and performing at local venues.
Race is a mix of the old and new - the new essence, a combination
of late 80s and early 90s themes done in the 21st millennium way.
He is like a loaded gun; he can go off at anytime. Come take a
ride on the soul side of the spectrum, walk with Race, hear and
see something new.

Discography

2016 - Five Star Morning
2015 - Gyrations
2014 - Baked Goods The E.P.
2014 - Sinsative
2012 - What If Jay Dee (Produced PCP)
2012 - The Mix Adventures Of Racetacula

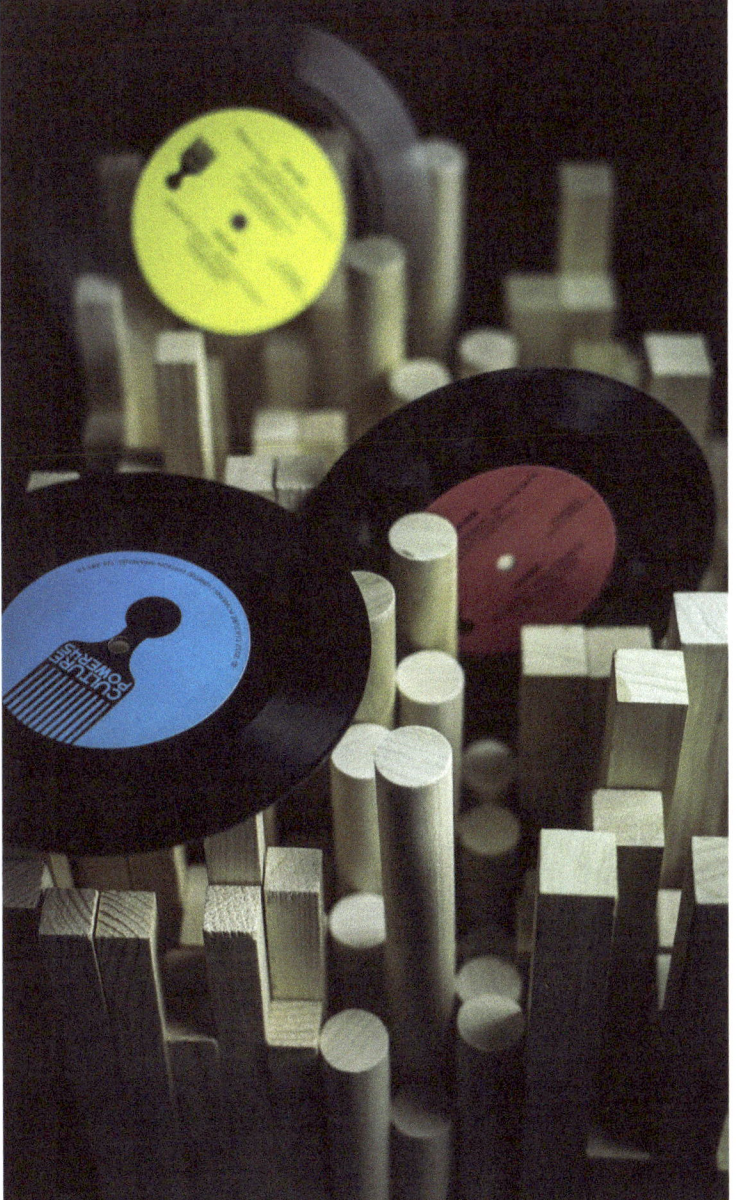

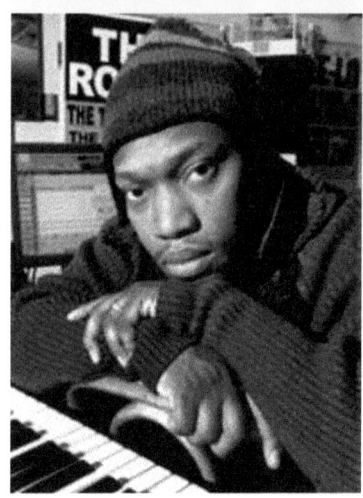

Kenautis Smith

ST LOUIS, MO

So why does he spend so much time in the basement? Even getting down there is tricky, if you're any taller than five-foot-six. Wires hang down from the ceiling, and the floor feels, in spots, like it's about to give out. Once you arrive at Smith's lair, you're greeted by a trifecta of vinyl: Jermaine Jackson's Let's Get Serious, The Story of Tron and an album that simply says Bootsy? on the cover.

"I just think they have interesting jackets," Smith explains. "It's not so much me liking the music that's on them."

His duties as the hardest-working producer in St. Louis hip-hop are what require Smith to spend so much time in this poorly lit dungeon. The girthy Jackson, Mississippi, native crafts beat after beat for local acts such as Coultrain, Black Spade and Jia Davis, and for regional acts who are finding their way onto the national radar, like Nite Owl, Juice and Qualo. The latter's latest release recently received three and half rabbit ears (out of four) from Playboy, and the magazine noted the album's "great production." Courtesy of River Front Times

Discography

Kenautis Smith - My Gift to the World (All Natural, Inc.)
Kenautis Smith & Blackspade Motivational Tool
Kenautis Smith & Race Bannon - "Five Star Morning

Production

Hi-Fidel And DJ Crucial - Traveling Between St. Louis And Chicago F5 Records 2001
Nite Owl - True Stories / Thief's Theme   2 versions Not On Label (Nite Owl Self-Released)2002 Soul Tyde - Soulful...ish (12") Uprising Music 2002
Soul Tyde - Hip Hop...ish (12") Uprising Music 2002
Jonathan Toth from Hoth - Brainwashing: The Art Of Hip-Hopera The Frozen Food Section 2002
Jerry G - No Question (12") F5 Records F5R009 2002
J.U.I.C.E. - Coronation (12") F5 Records F5R019 2004

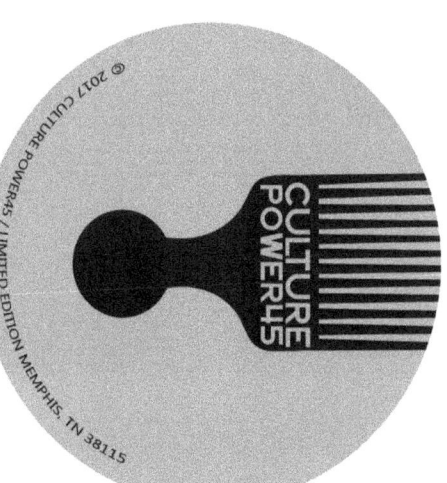

CULTURE POWER45

℗ 2017 CULTURE POWER45 / LIMITED EDITION MEMPHIS, TN 38115

CULTURE POWER45

THAT SIDE

80's BABIES (DEE JACKSON & TALL BLACK GUY) - Growth
Feat. Thalone Davis x Race Bannon
Produced by Tall Black Guy
Emannuelle's Theme Music (ASCAP)/Racetacular (ASCAP)

THIS SIDE

Edword Blackington
BlacKSkin x RedShirt x GraySquares
Produced by Waln & Knowboojo0
Egruss Music (ASCAP)

CP4505

WWW.CULTUREPOWER46.COM

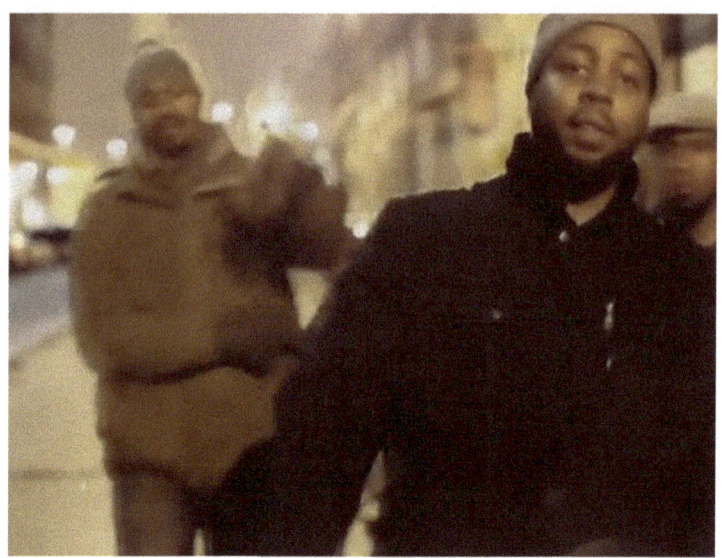

80's Babies

Tall Black Guy (DETROIT, MI)
Dee Jackson (CHICAGO, IL)

80's Babies is a rap group that consist producer Tall Black Guy
(Detroit, now UK) and rapper Dee Jackson from Chicago. They released a
new album called Searching For Happy and we talked about rapper Dee
Jackson about this great piece of music. We're a conscious hip-hop duo
formed in Chicago that embodies the true form of the culture. Well we're
both born in the eighties, but the eighties was also the growth and
development of hip-hop and represent that. So anyone can be an eighties
baby. I was born in the eighties but influenced by the early nineties .
I fell in love with hip-hop because of emcees like Nas, Tupac, Tribe
Called Quest and many more from that era, and their message was
conscious and love oriented for the most part. My parents also played a
major part by installing great morals and values in me.

Discography

Eighties Babies
Sonic Music
We Shall Not Be Moved
Searching Happy

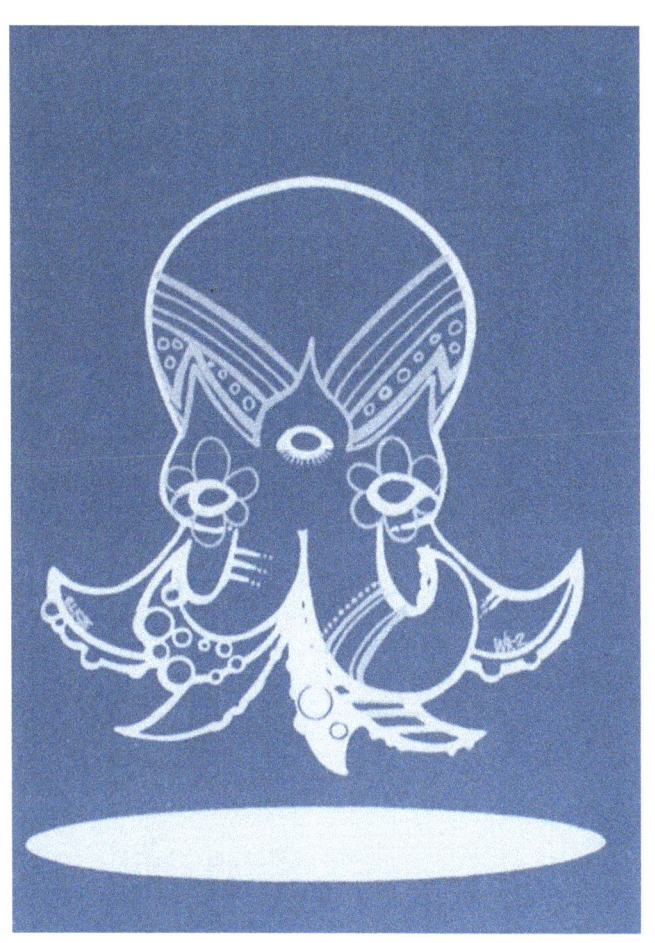

Edword
Blackington

ROSEWOOD, FL

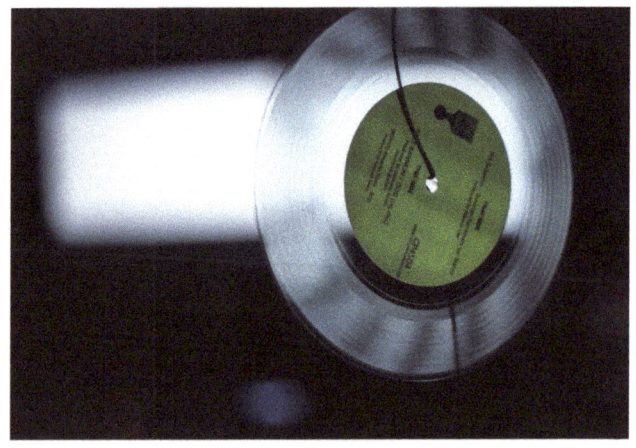

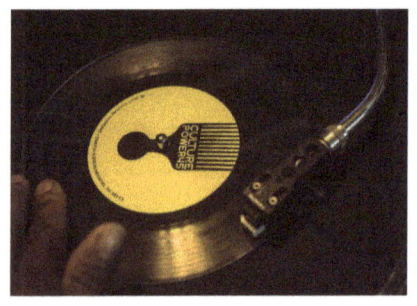

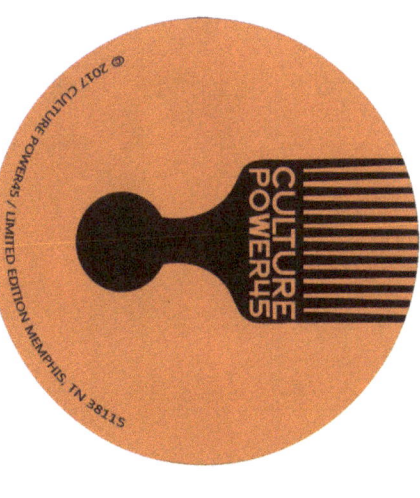

© 2017 CULTURE POWER45 / LIMITED EDITION MEMPHIS TN 38115

THAT SIDE

Fatnice - THIS (Remix)
Produced by Mr. Sonny James

Written by D. Jackson for Write On Brotha ASCAP
Produced by J Peterson for ill Worldwide ASCAP

THIS SIDE

Iomos Marad - Believas featuring iRonicLee
produced by Mozaic

Iomos Marad - Listen
produced by Mozaic

CP4506
WWW.CULTUREPOWER45.COM

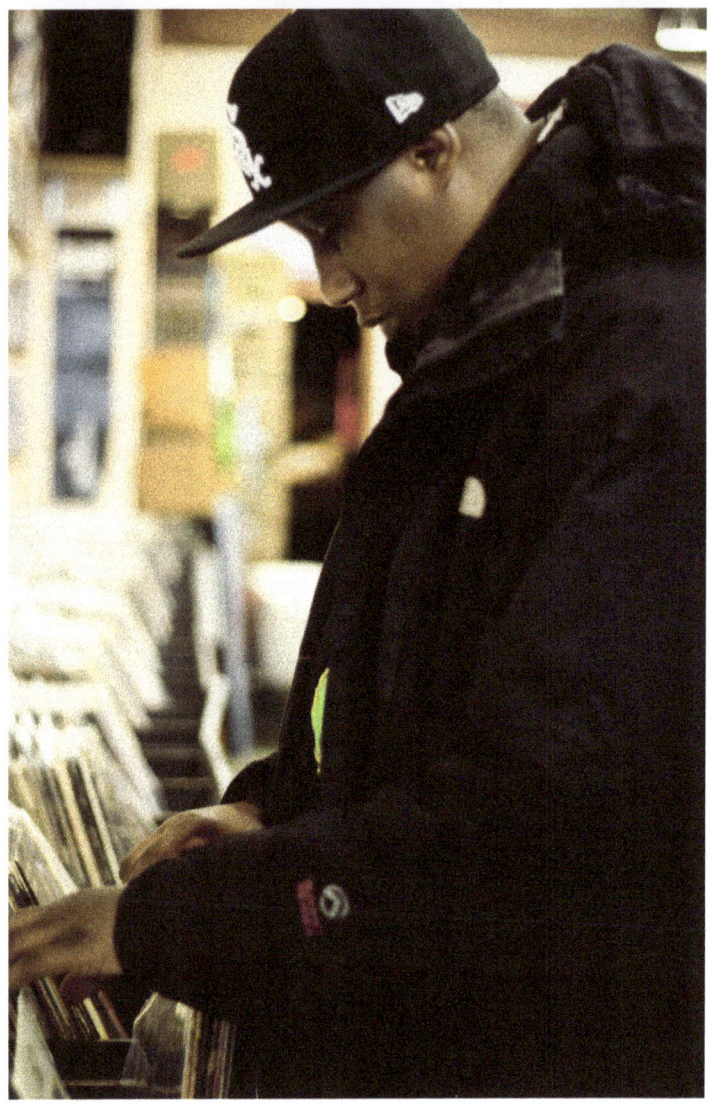

IOMOS MARAD

CHICAGO, IL

"Iomos Marad is a pure lyricist with a social agenda that educates and engages."
- XLR8R

"The sentiments stay solemn on Chicago drummer/MC Iomos Marad's"L.I.F.E." an
effecting, down tempo call for lost souls in the community to overcome adversity
through spirituality." - XXL

Iomos Marad (pronounced "eye-o-mahz" "muh-rod", but commonly referred to as I-O)
was raised in Chicago's Southside Englewood community and infamous 'Wild
Hundreds' by his mother, and life has not always been easy. His music pays
homage to her love, and the spirit of activism she instilled in him. His life
has been a unique spiritual journey and his rhymes reflect that depth of
experience. Standing 6' 3", Iomos casts a long shadow both literally and
figuratively. He walks tall through Chicago's rough streets to the beat of a
different drum...his own.

There is virtually no such thing as a 'one-of-a-kind' in hip-hop. A genre that
once took pride in originality has grown stale. Enter I-O ! Iomos built his
reputation the hard way...by rocking shows in Chicago's overcrowded underground
hip-hop scene. What set him apart from the beginning was his ability to play the
drums and rhyme...at the same time!!! By kicking clever freestyles while
delivering crisp strikes to the kick and the snare, Iomos has regularly stolen
the show while opening up for a variety of acts, including Mos Def, Slum
Village, Raekwon, Little Brother, Lupe Fiasco, The Hieroglyphics, Pete Rock,
Immortal Technique, Black Moon, just to name a few. He has also performed duets
with world famous sax player Frank Catalano. He has appeared on records with the
Molemen, Copperpot, Thaione Davis, Oddisee, J-Live and many others.

In 2003, Iomos released his debut album Deep Rooted on Chicago's 'All Natural,
Inc.' label. A critically acclaimed Hip Hop masterpiece, Deep Rooted was the
introduction of this Chicago veteran MC to the world at large. In 2006, he
followed up the success of Deep Rooted with his 9-track EP Go Head , another
favorite of Hip Hop enthusiasts. Iomos left 'All Natural' shortly after Go
Head's release, but has continued to record with various artists and rock shows
throughout the states and overseas; all while furthering his education and
earning a bachelor's in English Education.

Now, having achieved many of his goals personally and musically, he has found a
home among friends and fellow MCs at the indie label 'The Remnant Records'.
Looking forward to the future with Remnant, Iomos is even more committed to
impacting the culture of Hip Hop with God's truth through true skill and
lyricism.

DISCOGRAPHY

Albums

Deep Rooted All Natural Inc. 2003
The Meaning Of Marad (CDr, P/Mixed) All Natural Inc., The Hip Hop Project 2006
Go Head (CD, Album) All Natural Inc. AN-049-2CD 2006
Planting Seeds
Liberation the Voice EP (Album) What's the Irony? 2016

Singles & EPs

Deep Rooted (12", Single) All Natural Inc. IM-1 2000
L.I.F.E. All Natural Inc. 2002
Each 1 Teach 1 / Appetite 2 Write All Natural Inc. 2003
Don't Play Dat / If Ever / Beyond Space & Time (12") All Natural Inc. AN-049
2006
Stylin It (Single)

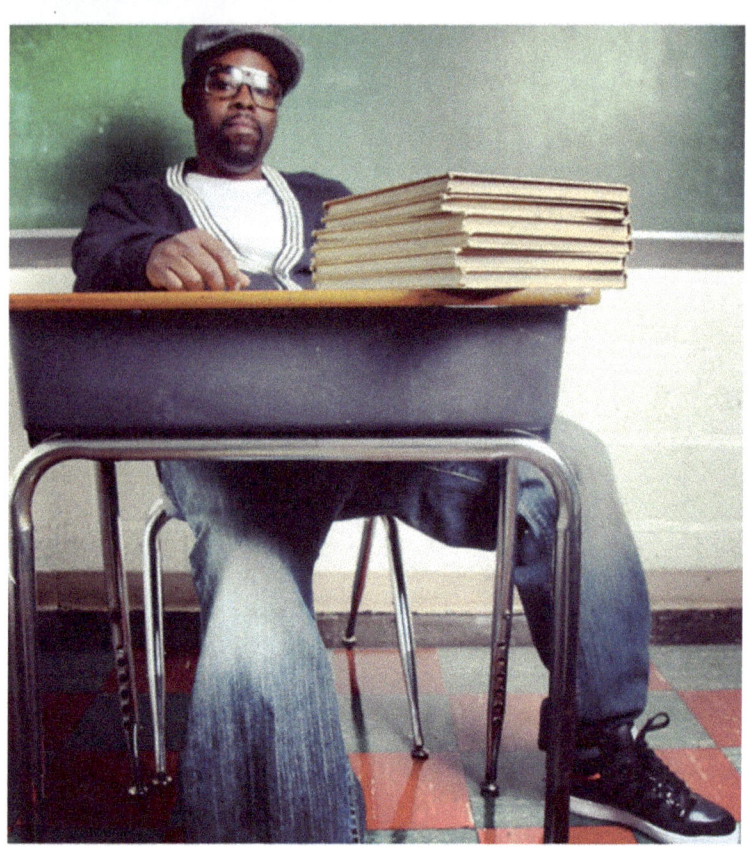

FATNICE

CHICAGO, IL / PHILLY

Fatnice found himself in Philadelphia, once again pursuing higher
learning and rocking open mics on the campus of The University of
Pennsylvania's' Veranda Room.   Shortly after his arrival Fatnice
linked with classmate Darin Tolliver (aka Gamez) and became a member
of Philly juggernaut Prophets of Ghetto having the honor of opening up
for the likes of Public Enemy and Dilated Peoples. Upon graduating
from PENN in 2000, Fatnice's decision to stay in Philly led him to a
life of recording and traveling internationally with the now defunct
Philadelphia based hiphop trio 84. Through 84 Fatnice had the
humbling experience of working with greats such as DJ Cash Money,
Bahamadia, Cee Knowledge of Digable Planets and a host of others.

Presently Fatnice, a true believer in the art of moving the crowd,
still performs, records and writes as well as flexing his vocal
talents under the alias Mojo Green. Along with his production partner
Blaak the 9th Man, the two have created Welcome To Soulville where
Fatnice releases material and produces. Fatnice also co hosts the
weekly podcasts Across The Tracks with Mr. Sonny James and Straight
From The Ville with Sammy Cook and Blaak The Ninth Man. To learn more
about Fatnice check out www.fatnice.com

Discography

2084 EP/84 (2001)
Ourselves LP/84 (2004)
Roddny Dangrr Fild LP/Infinito (2005)
Good Rap Music LP/ Bahamadia (2005)
It's Nice To Meet You CD/Casette) (2013)
Peace Love Unity and Havin Fun/Recordbreakin 45 (2013)
Ready To Rock Vol #2 (2014)
It's Nice To Meet You vinyl release/Chopped Herring (2015)
Ready To Rock Vol #2 (2016)
The Lost Tapes LP/Supavision (2016)
This (Remix) /Culture Power 45 (2016)

CULTURE
POWER45

© 2017 CULTURE POWER45 / LIMITED EDITION MEMPHIS, TN 38115

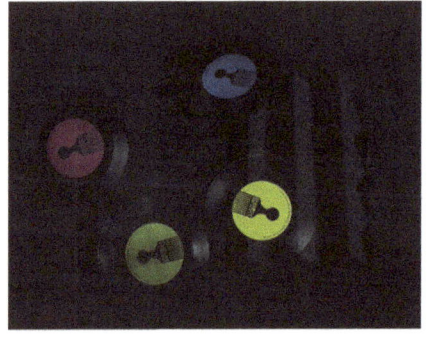

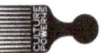

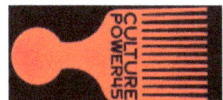

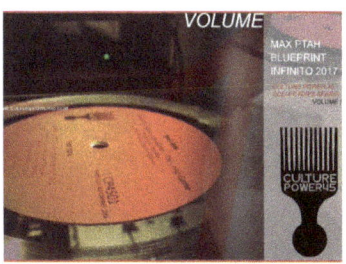

MAX PTAH
BLUEPRINT
INFINITO 2017
CULTURE POWER 45
COLLECTOR'S SERIES
VOLUME I

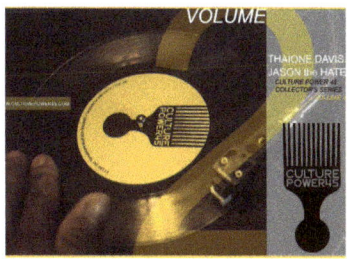

THAIONE DAVIS
JASON B's HATE
CULTURE POWER 45
COLLECTOR'S SERIES
VOLUME

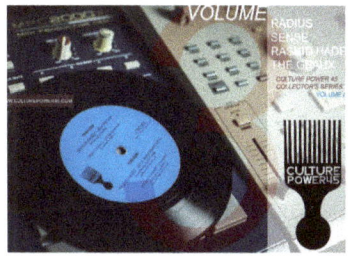

RADIUS
SENSE
RASHID HADEE
THE CRMX
CULTURE POWER 45
COLLECTOR'S SERIES
VOLUME I

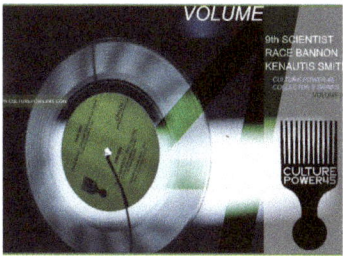

9th SCIENTIST
RACE BANNON
KENAUTIS SMITH
CULTURE POWER 45
COLLECTOR'S SERIES
VOLUME

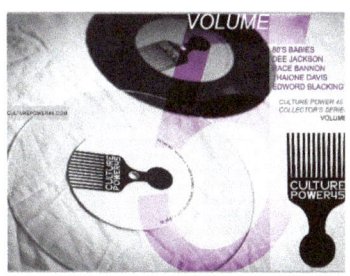

80'S BABIES
DEE JACKSON
RACE BANNON
THAIONE DAVIS
EDWORD BLACKING
CULTURE POWER 45
COLLECTOR'S SERIES
VOLUME

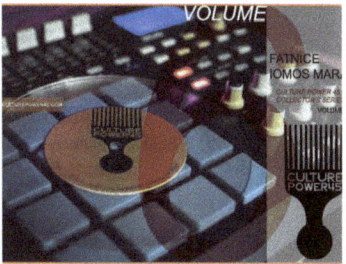

FATNICE
HOMOS MARY
CULTURE POWER 45
COLLECTOR'S SERIES
VOLUME